SYLVIA EARLE

BETH BAKER

In Consultation with Martha Cosgrove, M.A. and Reading Specialist

LERNER PUBLICATIONS COMPANY/MINNEAPOLIS

Martha Cosgrove has a master's degree from the University of Minnesota in secondary education, with an emphasis on developmental and remedial reading. She is licensed in 7–12 English and language arts, developmental reading, and remedial reading. She has had several works published, and she gives numerous state and national presentations in her areas of expertise.

Lerner Publications Company
A division of Lerner Publishing Group
241 First Avenue North
Minneapolis, Minnesota 55401 U.S.A.

Website address: www.lernerbooks.com

Library of Congress Cataloging-in-Publication Data

Baker, Beth.
    Sylvia Earle / by Beth Baker.
        p.   cm. — (Just the facts biographies)
    Includes bibliographical references and index.
    ISBN-13: 978-0-8225-3422-8 (lib. bdg. : alk. paper)
    ISBN-10: 0-8225-3422-3 (lib. bdg. : alk. paper)
    1. Earle, Sylvia A., 1935– —Juvenile literature. 2. Marine biologists—United States—Juvenile literature. I. Title. II. Series.
    QH91.3.E2B33   2006
    578.77'092—dc22   2005017037

Manufactured in the United States of America
1 2 3 4 5 6 – BP – 11 10 09 08 07 06

CONTENTS

THE BIRD LADY'S DAUGHTER

(Above) By 1970, Sylvia had a lot of experience as a deep-sea diver. She could calmly react to a stressful underwater situation.

IN 1970, THIRTY-FIVE-YEAR-OLD

Sylvia Earle was swimming deep beneath the surface of the Caribbean Sea. She was watching a fish eat tiny plants called algae. Suddenly, Sylvia realized she wasn't getting any air to breathe. The tube leading from her mouth to her scuba tank was blocked. She tried again to breathe in air. No air came through. She reached for the switch that let in the emergency supply of air. But the switch was broken.

Sylvia remained calm. She quickly guessed the distance between her and the underwater home she was sharing with four other scientists. Safety was a thousand feet away. This distance was too far to reach with only the air that remained in her lungs.

She quickly swam over to her dive partner, Peggy Lucas. Sylvia knew that every second mattered. She gave the "out of air" signal. This is a quick slicing motion with her finger across her neck. Peggy acted fast. She removed her mouthpiece and handed it to Sylvia. Sylvia breathed in a tiny puff of air. She stayed calm and passed the mouthpiece back to Peggy. In this way, the two divers shared the air supply as they swam safely back to their underwater home.

Sylvia had long been at home in the ocean. She didn't panic. Her skills as one of the world's most famous deep-sea divers helped her survive.

FALLING IN LOVE

Sylvia Alice Earle was born on August 30, 1935, in the town of Gibbstown, New Jersey. She was the second of Alice and Lewis Earle's three children.

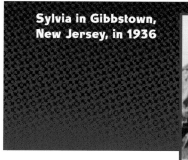

Sylvia in Gibbstown, New Jersey, in 1936

One of her first memories came in 1938, when she was three years old. She was playing in the ocean during the family's summer vacation. A great wave slammed the shore. The water knocked Sylvia down. Instead of crying, she got to her feet. She was ready to leap joyfully into the next wave. From that moment on, Sylvia loved the ocean.

That same year, the Earle family moved a few miles away to an old farm. It had a broken-down farmhouse that hadn't been lived in for a long time. The house didn't have water, electricity, or heat. The wind whistled through cracks in the windows. Nevertheless, Sylvia's parents had both been raised on farms. They wanted their children to grow up in the country too.

IT'S A FACT!

Bats lived in the Earle farmhouse, which local children thought was haunted.

The house had been built in the late 1700s, when George Washington was president. It was made from small bricks that had once been an old English ship. The house's nails and wooden beams were made by hand. And the kitchen fireplace was so big that Sylvia's father could stand in it. Lewis Earle was a good handyman. He put in the home's electrical wiring and the plumbing. After many months of hard work, the Earle family had a comfortable home. The house was filled with plants, animals, and noisy laughter.

Sylvia's parents never had much money. But they gave their children lots of time and energy. When Sylvia was small, her father asked to work the night shift. This way, he could spend mornings with his children.

THE BEAUTIFUL OUTDOORS

To Sylvia, the farm was the best place in the world. She loved to explore the farm's creek. She enjoyed the farm's old fruit trees that were knotted and twisted with age. Alice and Lewis added apple, pear, and walnut trees. They planted a huge garden, where they grew corn, tomatoes, beans, and asparagus. Sylvia and her brothers, Skip and Evan, helped harvest the crops. For a summer snack, Sylvia would pluck a green pepper from the garden. She'd cut off the top and dump out the

Sylvia and her brothers Evan *(left)* and Skip *(right)* sit in front of the fireplace writing letters to Santa.

seeds. The hollowed pepper made a nice bowl for fresh-picked berries. The farm had many colorful flowers and flowering bushes. Sylvia especially loved the lilac bush. She liked to hide under its drooping branches.

Sylvia was small for her age. She had straight, brown hair and a lively, eager face. She was always ready for an adventure. When she was five years old, her parents heard that a pilot was coming to town. The pilot offered rides in his airplane for a small fee. The family drove to a nearby field. There, a bright yellow plane called a Piper Cub sat with its propeller spinning. The plane had only one passenger seat. When Sylvia's turn came, she eagerly climbed aboard by herself. The plane swept up into the sky and took a few turns along the edges of Sylvia's town. She felt the air blow across her face and whip her hair. She looked down at the city below. The homes looked liked dollhouses. She could also see a few people.

Even better than the plane ride were the family's yearly trips to Ocean City, New Jersey. Sylvia and her brothers enjoyed chasing small sand crabs, collecting shells, and jumping in the waves. Sometimes they would see the sleek gray

IT'S A FACT!

At an early age, Sylvia learned to respect all living things. Sylvia's parents often brought pond frogs to their children. The children loved to look at the creatures and get to know them. Afterward, Alice and Lewis told the children to put the frogs back in the pond.

backs of dolphins rising out of the water far from shore. Television wasn't available when Sylvia was growing up. For fun, the children rode horses or went ice-skating or chased butterflies. At night, they played board games or drew pictures. Reading was also a favorite way to spend an evening. Sylvia's favorite books were true tales of adventure and stories about animals.

SYLVIA'S STUDIES

Another way Sylvia had fun was to look at pond life. At the pond, Sylvia would wait and watch for every little thing that happened. She tried to sit very still. The longer she was quiet, the greater the chance that she would see something interesting in the water. She kept a notebook at her side for sketching and writing down the things she saw and heard. No one had

Sylvia as a young girl

taught Sylvia how to collect scientific information this way. It was simply something she enjoyed. "I always knew, somehow, that I was going to be a biologist or a botanist, even before I knew what those things were called," she later said.

The house was filled with jars of Sylvia's collections. When her Aunt Maisie came to visit, she was disgusted by the jars of tadpoles, salamanders, and insects on the windowsills. She asked Alice why she let such things be in her kitchen. Alice just laughed. She was happy that her daughter loved plants and animals as much as she did. From the time Sylvia and her brothers were young, Alice taught her children to value and respect nature.

GENTLE ALICE

Alice's love of animals made her famous in the neighborhood. She became known as the Bird Lady for her gentle manner and healing skills. Alice had been a nurse. Children brought her injured birds and animals to heal. At one time, Alice nursed four orphaned squirrels. The squirrels looked like little balls of fluff to Sylvia. First, Alice fed the squirrels with an eyedropper. Then she showed Sylvia and her brothers how to feed the squirrels small pieces of bread dipped in milk. Later, the bread bits were dipped in peanut butter. In a few weeks, the children set the squirrels free. The young squirrels could now make their own way on the farm.

On autumn days, Sylvia and her mother took walks around the farm. Alice sometimes looked up at the sky and sadly remarked that the birds were disappearing. Alice didn't know why, but fewer birds seemed to be flying. Sylvia remembered a dozen little songbirds she had come across. The birds were all dead. Sylvia wondered what had happened to them.

Sylvia began to sense a change within the family. More and more, her mother had to nurse her little brother Evan. He was often ill with lung problems like bronchitis and pneumonia. Alice sat by Evan's side as he coughed painfully. Her father, too, was having problems. He was an electrician at a factory, but he no longer enjoyed his job.

When Sylvia was twelve years old, her family made a big change. Her father was unhappy with his job. The cold New Jersey winters were

IT'S A FACT!
Beginning in the 1940s, tons of pesticides were sprayed on crops to kill pests (insects). But the chemicals also were eaten by animals, such as birds. Alice and others saw the effects of pesticides and other chemicals on the environment.

hard on her brother's health. The family decided to move southward to Florida. The state was about 1,000 miles (1,609 kilometers) away from her beloved farm. "I didn't want to move at all," Sylvia recalled. "The woods, the pond, and fields were part of what I regarded as me." But her father decided to start a new business near his brother's home. And her mother thought the change in climate would help Evan.

CHAPTER 2

SYLVIA'S BACKYARD

ON A SUMMER DAY IN 1948, the Earle
family said good-bye to the farm. They piled
into the car for their move to Dunedin,
Florida. After several days on the road, they
drove down a dead-end street. Sylvia knew the
new house was near the Gulf of Mexico. The
Gulf is a huge section of the Atlantic Ocean.
But she was not prepared for what she saw.

Spreading out like a magic carpet was a giant blue
sea. Sylvia was thrilled. The ocean in New Jersey
was cold and gray. The ocean in Florida was bright
blue, warm, and calm. "That's when she lost her
heart to the water," her mother said.

For her birthday that year, Sylvia's parents
gave her a pair of swim goggles. With the new
goggles, she began her studies again. But instead of
a pond, she was studying the ocean. Sylvia floated
on the surface of the water. She peered down at
tiny crabs crawling in the sand beneath her.
Scallops hid in the sand. But Sylvia could see their
telltale bump and blush of
color. Hundreds of little
fish darted through the
grassy water. Sylvia was
amazed when a sea horse
floated by. "Having a

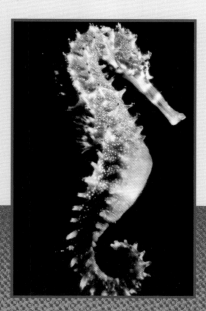

**When Sylvia's family moved to
Florida, she had the chance to
swim with sea horses (right)
and other marine creatures.**

chance to get acquainted with new critters was really a very good thing. It softened the blow of leaving the farm," Sylvia said.

SEA ADVENTURES

Sylvia gradually got used to her new home. She and her brothers explored the town of Dunedin. Tall oak trees lined the main avenues and shaded the streets. The children often went to the local drugstore. They bought Coca-Colas at the soda fountain. Sylvia soon discovered the town library. She loved sea adventures. Her favorite author was William Beebe. He was a biologist. In the 1920s, he had invented a way to go deep into the ocean in a round chamber called a bathysphere. In *Half Mile Down,* he wrote: "In this kingdom most of the plants are animals, the fish are friends." Beebe wrote about the marvels and wonders in the sea. He also said, "There may be a host of terrible dangers, but in hundreds of dives we have never encountered them." The words thrilled Sylvia. She longed to see the special creatures that Beebe described.

Sylvia and her brothers spent hours playing in the water. Sometimes Skip wanted to swim races.

THE BATHYSPHERE

In 1934, William Beebe *(right)* and Otis Barton went down to 3,028 feet (923 meters) below the ocean surface. No other human had ever gone down that far and lived. The two men had created a round vehicle called the bathysphere. Cables lowered the bathysphere into the sea. The men tested the temperature of the water at different depths. They also noted differences in the ocean's color.

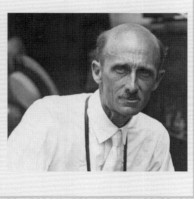

He swam well, and his arms cut cleanly through the water's surface. Sylvia tried to copy his smooth style. But she could not compete with him. Underwater was another story, however. There, she glided like a fish.

Sylvia's interest in nature continued to grow. In ninth grade, her science teacher, Edna Turnure, gave Sylvia great encouragement. "I loved doing special reports and making drawings of creatures. . . . I always had tons of extra credit," she remembered.

Sylvia's closest friend was Peggy MacKenzie. Peggy lived in a little house near the water. Sylvia walked to Peggy's house through the woods. Then they walked to Saint Joseph's Sound, one mile north in the Gulf. One day, as they drifted home, they noticed that something was churning the water, making it dull and cloudy. They followed the path of cloudy water to a pipe jutting from a new orange juice factory. The plant was dumping orange juice pulp into the clear water.

In Sylvia's opinion, the orange juice factory was only one of the ugly changes in town. Dunedin was growing fast. The beautiful old oak trees were being cut down. New hotels were being built. A seawall was being built to protect the new hotels from water damage. Sylvia wondered what would happen to the sea grasses and the tiny animals that lived in the ocean there.

In the spring of 1952, the end of high school was in sight. Because of her good grades, Sylvia was graduating a year early. She was only sixteen. (She would turn seventeen in August.) But Sylvia was growing restless. She felt there were more important things she wanted to do. She was anxious to get on with her life.

FIRST DIVE

That year, a school friend invited Sylvia and Skip to try out some diving gear. When it was Sylvia's turn, she slipped a heavy copper helmet over her head. The helmet's sharp edge dug into her shoulders. A hose linked the helmet to an air supply onshore.

Sylvia plunged into the water. She paddled downward and finally stood on the bottom of the river. She was 30 feet (9.1 meters) beneath the surface. She carefully edged her way out of the strong current. Suddenly, she spotted a school of small, golden fish. She slowly approached the fish. Sylvia expected them to swim away. Instead, the fish swam

Sylvia was fascinated with all kinds of marine life, such as these blackbar soldierfish.

to her. It was just as William Beebe had written about underwater creatures: "The joy of it all is that everything that moves has little or no fear of us."

After twenty minutes, Sylvia's vision began to blur. She felt like she might faint. Just as she was tugging on the air hose to signal that she wanted to come up, one of her friends dove down to get her. The air pump was not working properly. Sylvia had been breathing a deadly blend of carbon monoxide and other gasses. Her friends hauled her onto the riverbank just in time.

INSPIRED BY DR. HUMM

Sylvia got a chance to try new diving equipment called scuba gear. In 1953, when she was seventeen, she took a summer class about marine biology. The students would study the plants and animals that live in the ocean. Her instructor was Dr. Harold J. Humm. His love of the ocean deeply inspired Sylvia. Humm didn't tell his students to look at plants and animals under a microscope. Instead, he urged his students to go to see them as they live.

On their first field trip, Sylvia looked at Dr. Humm's equipment. She was thrilled. He had glass-bottom buckets, face masks, and flippers.

And, best of all, he had two scuba tanks. The sleek new gear was a big improvement over the clunky copper helmet she had first tried. On a boat, Dr. Humm took the students beyond the shores of Saint Mark's Wildlife Refuge. His instructions for using the scuba tanks were simple: "Breathe naturally."

DIVING IMPROVEMENTS

Ten years before Sylvia took her first dive, Jacques Cousteau and Emile Gagnan of France had invented the aqualung. The aqualung later became known as scuba *(below)*. This term came from the first letters of its definition—"self-contained underwater breathing apparatus." With scuba gear, a diver was able to explore and study the ocean. Cousteau and his team created other helpful diving tools, such as a one-person jet-propelled submarine, an underwater film camera, and an underwater home.

In his book *The Silent World*, Cousteau had written about his joy at exploring underwater caves and sunken ships. Scuba allowed him to swim with seals and sharks. Sylvia loved the book. She imagined herself flying through the water like Cousteau.

Sylvia explored the sea without fear. Those around her could see her enthusiasm for the world that existed in the deep waters.

Without fear, Sylvia jumped off the boat into a bed of sea grass. She gently kicked and glided to a small cluster of sponges. There she found an angry three-inch-long (8-cm) damselfish. The fish was not happy to see her in its territory. Sylvia balanced herself on one finger and easily lifted herself into a headstand. There, she could see into the fish's dark, cavelike hiding place.

Sylvia wished she could spend her life scuba diving. She wondered if she could follow in Dr.

Humm's footsteps and teach marine biology. For a teenage girl in the 1950s, this was an unusual career choice. The most common jobs for women were nurse, secretary, airline hostess, and teacher. Of these choices, Sylvia was able to imagine herself becoming a teacher. She could be like Dr. Humm and spend a lot of time in the water.

Focus on Algae

Sylvia went to college and studied hard, first at Saint Petersburg Junior College and then at Florida State University. Sylvia's parents couldn't afford to pay for college tuition. To make her way through college, Sylvia took out loans, worked part-time, and won scholarships.

After she graduated, she decided to pursue her master's degree. She was accepted at many top universities such as Yale, Cornell, and Duke. Sylvia decided to go to Duke University, in Durham, North Carolina. The school offered her two wonderful things. She won a full scholarship that would pay for all her schooling. And she also got to continue her studies under Dr. Humm, who was teaching there.

Harold Humm inspired Sylvia to focus her studies on ocean plants rather than ocean animals.

Humm taught her to look deeply at plants. "Plants provide shelter, whether it's underwater or above. They provide food. They provide the energy that supplies a whole interacting system," said Sylvia.

Alice and Lewis, still living in Dunedin, were very proud of their daughter's success. Alice began to babysit for children in the neighborhood. She sent her earnings to Sylvia to pay for her food. Sometimes Alice would send care packages of homemade skirts, blouses, and dresses. "I was the best-dressed person in school," Sylvia said proudly.

Sylvia's parents continued to encourage her dreams. She had endless energy. She began to believe she could become a scientist. During her two years at Duke, Sylvia decided to major in botany, the study of plant life. She focused her studies on algae. Some people think of algae as green scum or

IT'S A FACT!

Hundreds of types of algae live in the ocean. Some of Sylvia's favorite algae have a special feature called bioluminescence. Bioluminescence allows algae to send off their own light like fireflies do. A diver can see this light underwater.

Algae come in many different colors, such as the red algae above.

slimy seaweed. But Sylvia found algae amazing. "You'd have a hard time imagining plants so bizarre and absolutely magnificent. Algae could inspire poets and songwriters," she said. To learn about the plants, she spent many hours underwater. As she swam, she observed a magical world with shapes that resembled tiny fans, trees, spaghetti, and cacti.

BEING THE DOER

One thing clouded Sylvia's time at Duke, however. Not everyone wanted women to study science. She was often the only woman in her classes. When she signed up to be a teaching assistant, she was told that she would not be offered the job. She was told that such an job would be wasted on a female student. "Everybody knew" she would end up becoming a housewife. Sylvia was furious. She needed the money to pay for her living expenses and schoolbooks. How dare professors suggest that she was not serious about her studies?

Luckily, other professors appreciated Sylvia's hard work and intelligence. They created a new job for her in the herbarium. In this place, plant samples are kept for study. During this time, Sylvia decided that she did not want to be a teacher. "I wanted to do something that was different, something special," she said. "I had the impression that teachers taught about what others had done. But I wanted to be the doer. I wanted to do the finding, not just learn about what others had found."

3 AGE OF DISCOVERY

IN 1955, AT THE AGE OF TWENTY, Sylvia earned her master's degree. This higher degree spoke to her commitment to becoming a skilled marine biologist. That same year, she married Jack Taylor. He worked as a zoologist, a person who studies animals. After living briefly in Live Oak and Gainesville, Florida, Sylvia and Jack moved to Dunedin, next door to Alice and Lewis. After her marriage, Sylvia

(Above)
Sylvia on the beach in the mid-1950s

did not want to give up her dream of being a marine biologist.

Sylvia and Jack turned their garage into a laboratory. The lab had a microscope and cabinets to hold the specimens they found. Sylvia planned to get a Ph.D. degree through Duke University. Her research topic was algae in the Gulf of Mexico. She collected algae samples from the marshy grasses along the coast of Mississippi to the turquoise waters of the Florida Keys (an island chain off the coast of Florida). She measured the temperature and saltiness of the water. She recorded the depth of the water and its tides. She observed which plants and animals lived together.

In 1960, Sylvia and Jack's first child was born. Elizabeth was an active girl with strawberry blond hair. Two years later came baby John. The family called him Richie, after Alice's maiden name. Sylvia took the children along on trips in her boat. "Many times four small hands helped me arrange plant specimens on stiff, white sheets of herbarium paper and place them carefully between sheets of cardboard and blotting paper for drying," she wrote. This was a satisfying and peaceful time for Sylvia. She had her research, her children and husband, and her beloved parents.

DIVING DEEP

Only once have divers made it to the bottom of the ocean and come back. The Marianas Trench in the South Pacific Ocean is the ocean's deepest place at 35,800 feet (10,912 meters). This is about 7 miles (11 kilometers) down. In 1960, two divers made it to the trench and returned safely. Since then, no other divers have been successful. "Getting back is the real trick," says Sylvia.

Jacques Piccard (left) and Don Walsh (right) were the first and only divers to reach the bottom of the Marianas Trench.

ABOARD THE *ANTON BRUUN*

Then, in August 1964, she received an unusual invitation. A research ship called the *Anton Bruun* was working for the National Science Foundation. The ship was about to leave on a research trip to the Indian Ocean. At the last minute, one of the plant scientists was unable to go. Dr. Humm suggested Sylvia as a replacement.

Sylvia had every excuse to say no. Elizabeth and Richie needed her. She was studying for her exam to be accepted into the Ph.D. program at

Dr. Harold Humm *(left)* recommended Sylvia for the adventure on the *Anton Bruun.*

Duke. And her research in the Gulf of Mexico was going well. But her husband and parents told her that they would take care of the children during her six-week absence. Dr. Humm said she could take her exam early. And as for the Gulf of Mexico, it would still be there.

Sylvia decided to go on the expedition. But the *Anton Bruun*'s chief scientist told her that not everyone was happy about a woman being on board. A few of the men thought the idea of one woman traveling with seventy men was not a good idea. But Sylvia became more determined than ever to achieve her goal.

From the moment Sylvia walked on board

IT'S A FACT!

Some male scientists in the 1960s believed the old tale that women on ships make the sea angry and bring bad luck. Another old tale is that naked women on board calm the sea. This tale explains why figures of naked women are sometimes at the front of large ships.

the *Anton Bruun*, she knew she had to prove herself to the men. She was determined to work hard and to keep a sense of humor. For Sylvia, working hard meant doing what she loved best—exploring the sea.

The crew members of the 1964 voyage of the *Anton Bruun*

During the cruise, she got very little sleep. She rose at 5:00 in the morning to begin diving. She worked into the night. She wrote her observations in her journal at 3:00 A.M.

In unexpected ways, being the only woman on board had its advantages. For example, she was given her own small room. Most of the men had to share sleeping space. The men viewed her as the ship's "social ambassador." When the *Anton Bruun* docked at ports, Sylvia was invited to go ashore. Sylvia, the captain, and the chief scientist met with important local leaders. Sylvia would have preferred spending that time in the water. But she gained valuable experience as a spokesperson.

As much as possible, though, Sylvia was underwater seeing new critters, as she called them. She swam over tide pools, coral reefs, and mounds of black volcanic rock. She saw clown anemone fish, giant sea cucumbers, yellow butterfly fish, even a tiny octopus.

ONE FOR DR. HUMM

Once Sylvia came upon rocks covered "with a [tiny] forest of bright pink plants that appeared to have been designed by Dr. Seuss." She had never seen anything like it. The tiny plants looked like palm trees or umbrellas turned inside out. Sylvia had found a new type of red alga. As the person who first found it, she won the right to give it its scientific name. She called the pink plant *Hummbrella hydra*. This was a funny way to remind people of the alga's umbrella shape and to honor Dr. Humm.

Sylvia faced many challenges as the only woman aboard the *Anton Bruun*. Here, she relaxes on the deck of the ship.

Over the next two years, Sylvia went on four more research trips aboard the *Anton Bruun*. As her experience grew, she would have been a natural choice to become chief scientist. But many men still resisted the idea of a woman being their leader. "I decided I could either fret and get angry and bluster my way in. Or I could relax and enjoy the circumstances. I chose to not waste energy, but to do the best job I could," she said.

During this time, Sylvia got to know Eugenie Clark, a famous scientist known as the Shark Lady. Dr. Clark was a role model for Sylvia. Dr. Clark was a top researcher with her own lab. She was also a wife and the mother of four children.

THE SHARK LADY

As a child, Eugenie Clark had explored the aquarium at Battersea Park in New York. Soon after, she decided she'd become an ichthyologist (a scientist who studies fish). Like Sylvia, Eugenie graduated early from high school and earned her college degrees at an early age. She also had to deal with discrimination from her male colleagues. For example, they wanted to keep her off overnight research trips. They felt it wasn't proper for a female student to sleep in the same quarters as male students. Despite the setbacks, Eugenie went on to study many different types of fish, including blowfish, filefish, gobies, and sharks. Although Dr. Clark *(right)* worked with all types of fish, her most popular work was studying sharks. Her nickname, Shark Lady, came with the release of her book, *The Lady and the Sharks*. She was among the scientists that proved sharks could be taught to do different things, like pushing a button for food. In 1982, Clark made a film called *The Sharks*, which a huge number of TV viewers saw. Dr. Clark continues to devote her time to educating people about life in the ocean.

Sylvia wore a graduation gown, flippers, and goggles when she graduated with a Ph.D. from Duke University.

Sylvia was a frequent visitor to Dr. Clark's lab in Sarasota, Florida. The women often went diving together. Sylvia looked for algae, and Eugenie collected creatures for her lab. They used a small boat that had a well in the middle filled with seawater. They were able to keep fish and shellfish alive in the well. When Dr. Clark moved to New York in 1965, she asked Sylvia to oversee her lab. Sylvia worked in the lab until 1967. During this period, Sylvia earned her Ph.D. from Duke.

CHAPTER 4

DEEP-SEA ADVENTURES

AFTER NINE YEARS, Sylvia and John Taylor got divorced. She and her children then moved to Boston, Massachusetts. She later married Giles Mead. He was a leading ichthyologist at Harvard University. Between them, Sylvia and Giles Mead had six children. Sylvia had Elizabeth and Richie. Mead had three from an earlier marriage. Sylvia and Giles had a new baby, Gale, in 1968.

TEKTITE I AND TEKTITE II

The following year, 1969, the U.S. government began a series of experiments to study life in the sea. The first experiment was called Tektite I. It involved four scientists who lived for two months in a special laboratory on the floor of the ocean. The lab was 50 feet (15 meters) below the water's surface.

DIVING DANGERS

On land above ground, the air pressure a person feels is slight. And the pressure between the ear, throat, and lungs is the same. The pressure on land is in balance. Under the weight of water, the air pressure is out of balance. Divers get the pressure to a new balance by swallowing or blowing air from the nose gently. And the pressure increases the deeper a diver goes into the ocean. Going down slowly and coming back up slowly help ease the air pressure. If a diver rises too quickly, the diver can experience a sickness called the bends. This sickness can cause coughing, muscle pains, or even death.

The Tektite project was not only about marine life. The scientists at the National Aeronautics and Space Administration (NASA) also hoped to use some of the research in space. Aquanauts (sea explorers) and astronauts face similar problems. They both live in tiny spaces and explore strange environments. The name *Tektite* expressed this sea-space link. Tektites are green, glassy balls found on the ocean floor. Many scientists believe that tektites fell from space.

IT'S A FACT!

Sally Ride was the first U.S. female astronaut to go into space. Her first mission was in 1983, but she'd joined the NASA space program in 1978.

Sylvia learned about Tektite II from a bulletin board at Harvard. The bulletin asked scientists to submit ideas for underwater research. The planners of Tektite, however, did not expect women to apply. In those days, the idea of men and women living together in a science lab seemed improper or wrong. NASA also was not very interested in having women be part of the experiment. All U.S. astronauts at that time were men.

Several qualified women wanted to take part in the Tektite II study. But Sylvia's idea stood out from the rest. She was already doing research at Harvard. And she had more diving experience than any other person. Sylvia had a thousand hours of diving experience at that time. The planners decided to ask Sylvia to lead an all-female team.

IT'S A FACT!

Newspapers made a great fuss over the all-female Tektite team. The front page of the *Boston Globe* carried the headline: "Beacon Hill Housewife to Lead Team of Female Aquanauts." Sylvia groaned. She had done ten years of research to get her Ph.D. She had been on deep-sea research trips. But she was seen first as a housewife, not as a scientist.

Sylvia *(second from left)* and the other four women chosen for the Tektite mission had to go through many hours of training.

It would be hard for Sylvia to leave her family and her responsibilities at Harvard. But she didn't want to miss the Tektite opportunity. As always, Alice and Lewis offered to take care of the children.

UNDERWATER HOME

In 1970, Sylvia was sitting at a kitchen table, 50 feet (15 meters) under the sea. The carpeted room, painted a cheerful aquamarine, had a television and

a tape deck. Each bunk bed had a curtain that
could be pulled closed for privacy. Tucked into the
round walls were a refrigerator and a stove. NASA
provided frozen meals for the crew. Large
portholes—round windows—gave a fish-eye view of
the marine world surrounding the underwater
home. Fish sometimes stopped to gaze through the
lit windows.

The workstation was up a ladder from the
living area. The
station had a
laboratory and a
communications
panel. A short
tunnel led to the
life-support system.

**Sylvia does research
aboard Tektite II.**

A ladder in the tunnel led to a small room that opened to the sea. Inside, Tektite II was cozy and pleasant. But from the outside it looked grim—like twin oil tanks, standing upright on a concrete slab. Heavy cables ran from Tektite II to shore for communication and air. For seven months in 1970, the dwelling sat off the shore of the U.S. Virgin Islands. (The U.S. Virgin Islands are in the Caribbean Sea.)

Sylvia and her team of aquanauts swim off the U.S. Virgin Islands in July 1970.

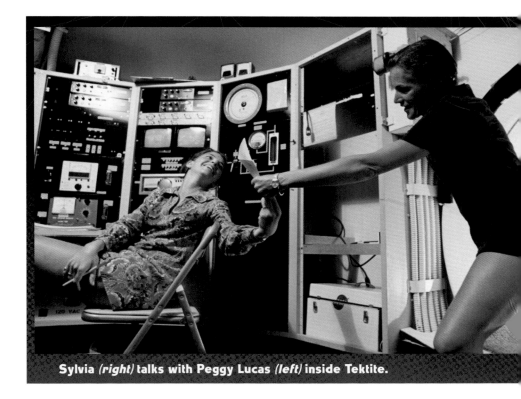

Sylvia *(right)* talks with Peggy Lucas *(left)* inside Tektite.

The women's team was called Mission 6. It was one of ten Tektite II missions. Sylvia was one of five people on the mission. Dr. Renate Schlenz True and Alina Szmant were marine biologists. Ann Hurley, an ecologist, would study how living things live together in the ocean. Peggy Lucas was a habitat engineer. Peggy's job was to see how the underwater home might be improved.

The blue chromis damselfish was one species studied by the Tektite crew.

Renate was there to learn if marine creatures could live in a bed of plastic grass. Farmers who raise fish for sale could use the plastic grass if it was successful. Ann and Alina studied the behavior of a type of fish called blue chromis damselfish. Sylvia's project was to study plant species growing in the reef (a ridge of coral or rock in the sea). Her goal was to learn how algae in the reef were affected by fish that lived and ate nearby.

The first day was not easy. The women had to get used to NASA scientists watching them twenty-four hours a day from television screens overhead. Every six minutes, each team member's activity was reported. Sylvia saw the humor of so many pairs of eyes watching one another. NASA was watching the women, who were watching the fish, who were watching the women. In turn, the women could stare back at NASA through the two-way television system.

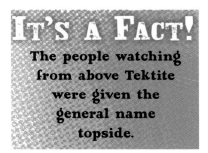

IT'S A FACT!
The people watching from above Tektite were given the general name topside.

By the second day, Sylvia was too excited about her work to be bothered by the ever-present eyes. She was eager to start exploring. She hoped the Tektite team would not change life for the plants and animals on the reef. She was pleased to see algae and worms clinging to the outside of Tektite II. They seemed to accept the ship as a normal part of ocean life.

A Typical Morning

The team's favorite time to go into the water was just before dawn. The women walked down the

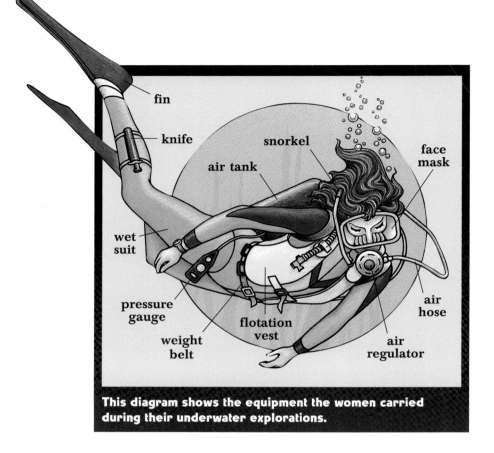

fin

knife

snorkel

air tank

face mask

wet suit

pressure gauge

flotation vest

air hose

weight belt

air regulator

This diagram shows the equipment the women carried during their underwater explorations.

ladder to the hatch (door). They wore their diving equipment. This included a weight belt to keep them from floating to the surface, a compass, a watch, a depth gauge, a knife, and a flashlight. They each also carried a yellow emergency balloon, a lantern, a collecting bag, and a waterproof writing slate. Along with their tanks, this gear was strapped around their waists, ankles, wrists, and backs or held in their

hands. When everyone was ready, Sylvia alerted the
topside that the women were setting out.

At last, they were free to enter the tropical sea.
The women swam quietly. They lit their way with
small flashlights. On a typical morning, Sylvia
headed for a spot where she could observe
damselfish guarding their eggs. At first, all was still.
But as daylight filtered down into the water, several
small damselfish appeared. They were sprinkled
with brilliant blue spots. They came out from a
coral patch where they had been resting. Dozens of

Sylvia shares samples with engineer Peggy Lucas, who is inside Tektite.

slender garden eels greeted the dawn. They pushed their small black noses out of their holes in the sand. They stretched their bodies upward and waved as gently as sea grass in the currents.

Other early risers included five gray angelfish. They came out of the same coral gap each morning. What Sylvia loved most about living underwater was becoming familiar with individual

IT'S A FACT!

The salt in seawater can eat away at equipment. Washing everything—bodies and equipment—in freshwater stops the salt from damaging anything.

fish and observing how they behaved. The hour passed quickly. The air in the scuba tanks ran low. It was time to return to Tektite II. One by one, they swam into the pressurized chamber. They climbed up the ladder to unload their gear. They took turns bathing in the freshwater shower. Sylvia let topside know that they were back safely.

UNUSUAL SOUNDS AND SIGHTS

After a short rest, Sylvia would grow restless. Every minute spent out of water seemed like a waste of time. One afternoon, she and Renate set out. This time, they were using rebreathers instead of scuba tanks. Rebreathers were a new invention. They cleaned the diver's air and removed dangerous carbon dioxide. Rebreathers took longer to prepare for use. But they had many advantages. With rebreathers, divers could remain in the water for much longer–four wonderful hours. This was enough time to accomplish what would take three separate trips with scuba gear. The rebreather is quieter than scuba because it

The Tektite II all-female team in rebreather training

makes no bubbles. The women could hear all the
sounds from the sea—"the crunch of parrotfish
teeth on coral, the sizzle and pop of snapping
shrimp, the grunts of groupers, the chattering
staccato of squirrelfish," Sylvia wrote.

That afternoon, the first stop was Renate's
field of plastic grass. Algae covered the strands of
plastic grass. This was a good sign that fish might
soon be eating there. The two women next glided
over the smooth ocean floor to one of Sylvia's
study areas. Sitting on round rocks, they watched
the action on the reef. Just then, a small,
snakelike lizardfish swam near. It rested on
Sylvia's flipper. Later, they spotted a batfish, an
odd-looking, sand-colored animal with armlike
flippers for walking on the ocean floor. To
Sylvia's surprise, the batfish allowed Sylvia to cup
it in her palm. When the fish began to wriggle,
she let it swim away.

Frequently, the women swam at night.
Swimming in the pitch-black sea might frighten
most people. But it offered the divers a chance to
see different fish. Darkness brought out the octopus,
which changed colors from brown to blue green as
it hunted its prey. Shining creatures winked like

Swimming in the darkness at night allowed Sylvia to see creatures that may not be out during the day.

fireflies in the darkness. Moonlight shone on the ocean floor.

SAYING GOOD-BYE

Far too soon, the two weeks were up. Sylvia and Ann swam out together to say good-bye to the reef. As if on cue, the five gray angelfish appeared. The women gathered some algae to bring back to the doorway of the dwelling. Placing the algae on the seafloor, they waited to

see if any fish would eat this easy breakfast.
Sylvia kept a small sample of algae for her
collection. Soon, parrotfish showed up to munch
on the pile of algae. Then an angelfish came. To
Sylvia's delight, the fish began eating a piece of
algae she held in her hand. When the women
heard the diving bell, they knew it was time to
leave. They began their final swim.

Sylvia's research had gone well. She had
observed 154 species of marine plants. She had
found 26 species never seen before in the Virgin

The Tektite team. Sylvia is at the far right.

Islands. She had also made new observations about the day and night behaviors of many plant-eating fish. The other team members were also pleased with what they had learned. Renate's bed of plastic grass created a good habitat (living space) for fish. Ann and Alina learned more about the escape behaviors of the blue chromis damselfish. Peggy found the living quarters of Tektite II were well-made, but the laboratory space was too small.

SUDDEN FAME

Meanwhile, reporters eagerly waited for the group to return to shore. They were excited by the idea of the all-female team. Earlier Tektite studies had not received much attention from reporters. But this time, an enthusiastic crowd clapped when the women stepped onto the pier. As cameras snapped, each team member was given a bouquet of red roses. That was just the beginning.

In Washington, D.C., the women spoke before the U.S. Congress and received awards. First Lady Pat Nixon invited them to lunch at the White House. Later, in Chicago, Illinois, they rode in a parade in a fur-lined limousine to a reception at the

Shedd Aquarium. There the famous gospel singer Mahalia Jackson sang for them.

But the female scientists had mixed feelings about their sudden fame. It was exciting to be famous. But it also made them uncomfortable. None of the other Tektite scientists had been treated as stars. And the headline writers dreamed up silly names for the team, such as "aquanettes," "aquabelles," and "aquababes." The writers wouldn't have called male scientists such silly names. But some of them didn't like all the attention the women received.

Sylvia's standing as a respected scientist seemed in danger of drowning in a media wave. But at the same time, something important was happening. Well-known TV reporters such as Barbara Walters and Hugh Downs wanted to interview her. She was asked to give speeches at clubs, companies, and schools. Sylvia knew that people didn't just like her because she was a brilliant scientist. The fact that she was a "girl" explorer was what made her popular with the press. This gave her a way to reach millions of people with her message. As microphones were thrust before her, she searched for the right words to express how deeply she felt about life in the oceans. Her role as a public champion of the seas had begun.

"I'm changed forever because I lived underwater for two weeks in 1970. I wish that everybody could go live underwater if only for a day," she later said. She was convinced that the more people knew about life in the sea—not just by reading about it but by seeing it for themselves—the more they would value it and want to take care of it.

For Sylvia, the 1970s were a time of great discovery and hope. The first national marine sanctuary was set up in 1975. The sanctuary is

Sylvia viewed sea life with amazement. She felt if more people could see what she saw, they would care more about protecting the ocean.

like an underwater national park. Within the sanctuary's boundaries, ocean plants and animals are protected from harm. Sylvia imagined that marine biology students of the future would study in underwater laboratories. She was sure an exciting age of ocean research was about to begin.

CHAPTER 5
GENTLE GIANTS

SYLVIA SAT BALANCED ON THE EDGE
of a small rubber boat. She was excited and
nervous. Her heart felt like it was in her throat.
Below her, in the warm Pacific Ocean waters
off Hawaii, swam humpback whales. These are
some of the largest animals in the world. In
1977, few people had the courage to swim with
humpback whales. The creatures are huge.
They can kill a human with a single stroke of
a flipper or tail.

(Above) In
1977, Sylvia
and a crew
began to
learn more
about
humpback
whales.

Sylvia slid into the water. Under the surface, a black form came hurtling toward her like a fast train. For one horrifying moment, she wondered if she'd made a terrible mistake. She was a small person who didn't weigh much. Yet she was up against a 40-ton whale. A crash seemed certain. But the whale gracefully slid past her. It tilted its enormous head to get a better look at this bold little visitor. Sylvia felt a thrill. She recognized something in the whale. She had met a new friend who seemed to share her curiosity and joy.

Sylvia turned toward her dive partners, photographers Al Giddings and Chuck Nicklin. She realized Giddings was about to have an even closer encounter with the same whale. Giddings had no idea that the whale was heading right for him. There was no way Sylvia could warn him. But at the last second, the whale swam just over Al's head. "I stopped worrying then and have never worried since in all my encounters with humpbacks," Sylvia wrote in *National Geographic.*

THE LANGUAGE OF WHALES

Human hunters know all about dead whales. But little is known about living whales. Roger and Katy

Payne are two scientists who worked to change that situation. After years of research, the Paynes learned that whales compose songs in their own kind of whale "language." The songs change each year and are shared by other whales in the pod (group of whales).

Sylvia met Roger Payne at a conference. They decided to work together on a research project. The highlight of the project would be a film made by Al Giddings, a pioneer in underwater photography. Sylvia was delighted. She and Giddings shared a fearless passion for underwater exploration. And they had worked together on many expeditions around the world. To raise money for the whale project, they talked to scientific organizations, magazines, and conservation groups. They explained that very few scientists had done whale research by swimming alongside the giant animals. They convinced

IT'S A FACT!

Studies show that whale songs are a collection of individual noises. The whales use the noises to communicate. They remind scientists of human singing. The songs take place during winter, when male whales are trying to attract a female mate.

several organizations to give money to help pay for the film.

In February 1977, they began the project in Hawaii, where humpback whales travel in the winter. By the second day of filming, the whales already seemed to expect the crew to show up. Five black forms swam past the crew's boat. The whales turned around and swam back toward the boat. Sylvia didn't hesitate. She plunged in. Two whales immediately swam to her from below.

The crew followed the humpbacks for three months. Sylvia learned to recognize individual whales by the markings on their faces, flippers, underbellies, and flukes (tails).

WHALE HUNTING

Humans have hunted whales for centuries. In 1880, only about fifty whales were killed each year. Whalers hand threw long spears, called harpoons, at whales. Modern machinery brought whaling to an all-time high. By the 1930s, more than fifty thousand whales were killed each year. Harpoons were fired from guns that carried explosives. Factory ships floated on the sea. There, whales could be more easily butchered and ground into animal feed, lard, and cosmetics. "In less than a century we have traded 60 million years of history for margarine and cat food," Sylvia wrote. Much of the whale hunt has been banned. But many kinds of whales—including the humpbacks—are still endangered.

One of the most exciting days came when the crew crossed the Alenuihaha Channel. This stretch of water runs between two of Hawaii's islands. The channel is difficult for boats to cross. Winds blow fiercely there. The current is strong. That day was stormy. The waves were 30 feet (9.1 meters) high.

Everyone clung to the boat as towers of water rose and fell around them. Just then, they saw an unusual sight: pygmy killer whales were interacting with the humpbacks. The storm was dangerous. And no one had ever swum with the aggressive pygmy killer whales. But Al and Sylvia decided to go into the water to film them.

Roger Payne remembered the scene this way: "It's utter turmoil. Everything is violent. And you can't see where water and air begin. The second

IT'S A FACT!

Humpback whales are migratory. This means they move long distances in summer and winter. In summer, they tend to be in the cooler ocean areas, such as the waters of Antarctica. They use the summer months for massive feeding. In winter, the whales do not eat. Instead, they travel hundreds of miles to warmer waters. In winter, the whales either mate or give birth.

Sylvia and Al went into the water, you couldn't see their bubbles [from their scuba tanks] at all. The waves were breaking into the boat."

Sylvia and Al made five dives. After the third dive, they came up to change a piece of equipment. Sylvia said to Al, "Did you see those sharks?" The people on board were impressed. Sylvia wasn't worried about the sharks at all.

Two large ocean white-tipped sharks had approached Sylvia. One had circled her. Then it had moved in as if to attack. Sylvia gave a sharp kick of her flippers, and the shark swam away.

Sylvia saw white-tipped sharks *(above)* while swimming with whales in Hawaii.

Sylvia aboard the boat on the whale mission in Hawaii

Roger Payne continued: "Did Sylvia and Al go back in? Absolutely! Did they have anything to protect themselves? Of course not! That is very, very typical. Sylvia has more guts than almost anybody you can name."

SHARED ADVENTURES

By the late 1970s, Sylvia and her family had moved to Oakland, California. There, Sylvia had done research through the California Academy of Sciences. Her second marriage had ended. Sylvia felt sad about the divorce. Her own parents were still devoted to each other. She admired their strong marriage. But it was as if Sylvia were wed to the sea. She was devoted to her ocean work. This probably put a strain on her relationship.

Alice and Lewis often came to California to care for the children when Sylvia was on her trips. But Sylvia shared many of her adventures with her children. Elizabeth, Richie, and Gale had all learned how to scuba dive when they were young. Sylvia sometimes let them stay out of school to go with her on her trips. In fact, she brought her children with her on the Hawaii whale trip.

Elizabeth, who was seventeen, was given a big responsibility on the whale project. She had to ride in the black rubber boat and take care of the expensive underwater cameras. When the crew needed a piece of equipment, she carefully handed it over the side. All of a sudden, the boat tipped up on one end. A whale was lifting the boat out of the water!

Elizabeth was shocked. "All around the boat was nothing but whales. It was like the whale was playing with the boat. I was so nervous–what would I do if the boat got tipped over? I wasn't worried for me—the whales were so gentle—but I was supposed to be keeping the equipment dry!" Luckily, the whale soon tired of this game and left her alone.

Sometimes the whales would sing. Their songs were full of deep bass moans and high squeals. During the filming, Al Giddings was the first person ever to take a picture of humpbacks singing. As the whales sang, Sylvia and the children got in the water. The music was loud and strong.

A humpback whale calf (baby) and its mother make their way through the water.

Sylvia enjoyed watching whales play.

In the film, *Gentle Giants of the Pacific,* Sylvia swims gracefully around the whales. Her light brown hair streams around her snorkel mask. The whales are just as graceful. Their tons of blubber do not keep them from smoothly gliding and twisting through the water. Their powerful tails churn clouds of foam.

Sylvia put the film to good use, showing it in twenty countries. Her audiences shared with her the thrill of seeing whales singing, romping, and caring for their young. Humpback whales, she said, swam in her dreams forever. They brought a grin to her face when her mind wandered during a boring meeting. Swimming with such wonderful animals inspired her to speak out more strongly than ever to protect the critters who live in the seas.

CHAPTER 6

A WILD AND CRAZY IDEA

IN 1979, AL GIDDINGS came to Sylvia
with an idea for a new adventure. How would
she like to take a walk in an aquasuit along the
deep ocean floor while Al filmed her? Sylvia
had doubts. She had seen pictures of the
aquasuit. It was called a Jim suit, after Jim
Jarrett. He was the diver who had worn an
earlier version of the suit in 1920. Divers wore
the bulky Jim suit to do underwater chores,
such as ship repairs. Sylvia and other divers
called the suit Jim.

Sylvia liked the freedom of moving through the water in lightweight gear. She enjoyed gently touching the plants or sometimes even a fish. Wearing Jim underwater would be like dancing ballet in a suit of armor. Jim's metal, clawlike hands would probably crush a delicate piece of coral.

But Al wanted people to see Sylvia walking on the ocean floor. They would get a better understanding of deep-sea exploration. Images from the film of her walk could be used in their next book, *Exploring the Deep Frontier*. He and Sylvia were also working on a television special for the National Geographic Society. The film could also be used for that show.

If she were willing, Sylvia would be the first scientist to use Jim. Sylvia thought about the offer. In Jim, she could be dropped into the ocean for a few minutes or hours. She could see the suit as an unusual "lab coat"—after all, the ocean was her laboratory. Sylvia accepted the job. Al was not surprised that Sylvia was unable to turn down the challenge. When had she ever said no to a deep-sea adventure?

CLOSE TO THE EDGE

Al then needed to hire a team of scientists to go with Sylvia. The first was Phil Nuytten of Oceaneering

International, Inc. Phil was the owner of all fifteen
Jim suits. He knew that Jim might be useful to
scientists. Phil was especially excited that Sylvia
would be using Jim in a new way. In the past, Jim
divers had been attached securely by a heavy cable
to a platform on the surface of the water. Sylvia
would be linked only by a slender cord to a small
underwater vehicle called a submersible. The
submersible would allow her to go deeper in the
ocean, perhaps to 1,500 feet (457 meters). She would
be freer to explore. "Some might regard [this] as
dancing too close to the edge of safe and sane
diving," Sylvia wrote. "Phil and Al seemed
uncommonly attracted to wild and crazy ideas."

Others were not so delighted. Graham
Hawkes, a British marine engineer, was asked to
judge the project's risks. Hawkes was worried
about the possible dangers. Still, after careful
study, he determined that the expedition would
probably be safe.

Dr. John Craven, director of the University of
Hawaii's Marine Science Institute, did not agree
with Hawkes. Craven was responsible for *Star II*,
the submersible that could transport Sylvia to the
bottom of the sea. "No. Impossible. The risks are

too great," he declared. But Hawkes was able to convince Craven that the project was safe.

The final task was raising money for the operation. Al and Sylvia gathered funds from National Geographic and other sources. Jim was taken apart and put back together again to make it fit Sylvia's small body. Hawkes worked to make Jim's joints more flexible in the deep ocean.

The Jim suit looked like a space suit. But unlike a space suit, an aquasuit must be made of tough material, such as ceramic or metal. If the suit isn't tough, the diver would be crushed under the heavy pressure of the ocean. Remember, the deeper a diver goes, the more the pressure. Jim was made of a

The Jim suit hangs from *Star II* during a practice run.

Sylvia smiles through the head of the Jim suit.

light but tough metal called magnesium. The suit looked like an overweight white caterpillar. The suit's thick arms had big round elbow and wrist joints and steel grippers. The tree-trunk legs had round knee and hip joints and big black boots.

To put on the suit, Sylvia tilted the headpiece forward. She then climbed in from the top. She could look through four round plastic portholes in the headpiece to see all around. Gauges inside the suit showed her the water's depth and the oxygen level.

Sylvia trained hard for one week. First, she wore the Jim suit in a big tank and then in shallow

Sylvia gets into the Jim suit.

water near shore. She had trouble walking, so weights were added to Jim's feet. Even with the weights to hold her down, Sylvia was standing on her toes to walk. The suit was big enough for her to easily move her arms to take notes. Sylvia lurched around the training tank. She said she felt like a walking refrigerator. At last, all was ready.

THE JIM DIVE

The tiny yellow submersible *Star II* descended into the Pacific Ocean on October 19, 1979. Two times earlier, the sub's efforts to go down had failed. But this time, *Star II* carried its strange cargo. Sylvia was inside the metal Jim suit. She was strapped awkwardly around the waist and was on a platform at the front of the sub.

As the sub sank deeper, Sylvia looked out at the constantly changing blue water surrounding her. She wanted to remember every moment of this journey. It was the most dangerous and exciting adventure of her life. For two and a half hours, she would walk across the deep ocean floor, where no human had ever stepped before.

Watching with Al Giddings was Bo Bartko. He was a highly experienced submersible pilot. Sylvia heard Al's voice saying they had reached 1,000 feet (305 meters). After two failures, her hopes grew. Perhaps this would be the day.

The sky blue water turned to gray and then to midnight blue. Tiny glimmers of light sped by her helmet, like moths on a summer night. Her pulse quickened with excitement.

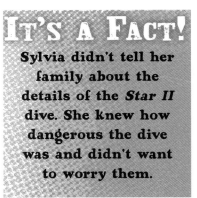

IT'S A FACT!

Sylvia didn't tell her family about the details of the *Star II* dive. She knew how dangerous the dive was and didn't want to worry them.

Sylvia begins her descent into the ocean in the Jim suit.

They were at 1,150 feet (350 meters) under the water. Bo brought *Star II* down with a gentle bump on the sandy sea floor. In the glow of the headlights, Sylvia saw some slender branches of coral. Glassy shells of red shrimp were scurrying across the seafloor. She was so eager to begin that she tried to take a step. For a moment, she forgot she was still attached at the waist.

Sylvia was anxious to begin her explorations. But she asked Bo to go deeper. She wanted to find a spot with more coral or rocks that would attract more fish. For another half hour, Bo guided the submersible. At last, at 1,250 feet (381 meters), he said the time for searching was up. The sub's power supply was running out. Sylvia peered out at a marvelous seascape. She realized that they had found an ideal spot.

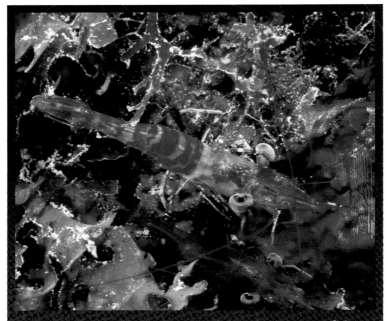

Red reef shrimp, shown here at night, where some of the many colorful creatures Sylvia came across while diving.

It was up to Al Giddings to turn the lever and release Sylvia. This was the most difficult thing he had done in all his ten thousand dives. Sylvia and the crew had followed careful safety measures. But the dangers were many. If Sylvia got into trouble at this depth, Al would be unable to safely leave the sub to help her. He kept his voice calm as he asked Sylvia if she was ready to go. Sylvia replied just as calmly, "Any time."

Al turned the lever. A problem arose immediately. To Sylvia's dismay, Jim's toe was stuck on the platform of *Star II*. Could she be this close to her historic walk and have to give up the mission?

Bo thought he could jar Sylvia loose by speeding up and quickly moving the sub backward and forward. He shot the sub in reverse. After one try, the boot became unstuck. At last, Sylvia was free to roam—or as free as someone in a heavy metal suit can be.

A LIGHT SHOW

Sylvia slowly, awkwardly moved forward. She felt like astronaut Neil Armstrong taking the first dramatic step on the moon. But the moon has no life on it. In the ocean, Sylvia discovered a world bustling with life, even at this crushing depth.

   She admired a dozen long-legged scarlet crabs. They clung to the branches of a delicate pink coral. Gleaming jellyfish drifted by like bubbles from a wand. Flat, diamond-shaped fish called rays hovered off the ocean floor. The rays were 7 feet (2 m) long, larger than any Sylvia had ever seen. They rippled their rubbery wings.

Sylvia walks on the ocean floor.

Many different rays live in the ocean. This is a southern stingray.

As Sylvia walked, she jotted down what she saw. A small shark with bright green eyes glanced in her direction. Looking confused, the shark hit a stalk of coral. Then it glided away. Sylvia knew that *Star II*'s lamps seemed dim to those who walk on land. But they must have seemed as bright as floodlights on a baseball field to creatures whose eyes had never seen the sun. She asked Al to turn off the lights. Some of the creatures around her were bioluminescent. This meant they produced their own natural light. Sylvia was plunged suddenly into darkness. Her eyes took a few minutes to adjust.

Sylvia looked up through the top porthole of her suit. She focused on the bizarre and wonderful creatures around her. A lantern fish swam by. Its even band of tiny yellow lights glowed like the windows of a passing train in the night. She stopped to watch a silvery hatchetfish. The fish's eyes sat on stalks, glaring upward. Another part of its body looked like a car's headlights beaming

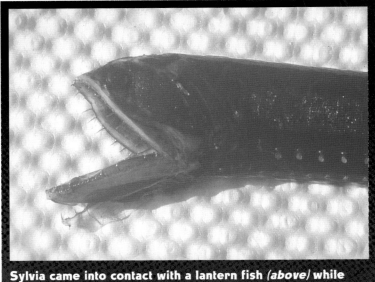

Sylvia came into contact with a lantern fish *(above)* while exploring the ocean floor in the Jim suit.

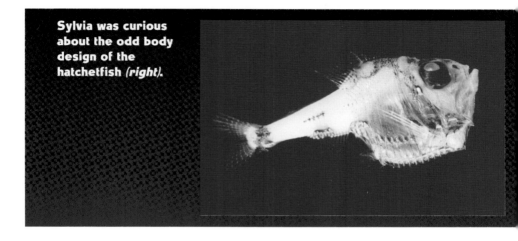

Sylvia was curious about the odd body design of the hatchetfish *(right)*.

downward. Suddenly a light show of blue burst beside her. She was standing among hundreds of slender, coil-like colonies of bamboo coral. "The most gentle nudge of my claw provoked ring after ring of blue light to pulse . . . down the full length of the coral," she later wrote. When she touched the bottom stalk, the same light show occurred. Fiery blue rings passed upward and through those rippling down.

Sylvia wrote furiously in her notebook. Her mind raced with questions. What was the purpose of the gleaming rings of blue? Were they a signal warning off other animals? Or were they lights to attract prey? Her thoughts were interrupted by Al's voice telling her the time was up. "You're kidding!" Sylvia cried. "It seems like 20 minutes." She slowly shuffled back to the sub.

RECORD BREAKER

Reluctantly, Sylvia told Al and Bo to begin the climb up to the surface. The sub rose slowly back through the changing shades of blue. Sylvia dangled from the cord. When she emerged, she took her place in the record books. The Jim suit would soon be outdated. Smaller submersibles would make it much easier for scientists to explore the ocean. No one would again walk as deeply on the ocean floor as Sylvia had done. Newspapers from around the world reported on her Jim suit dive. Al's pictures were printed in many books. Together Sylvia and Al produced a television special.

Sylvia remains a legend to many divers.

IT'S A FACT!

Using the suit's pincers, Sylvia planted two flags on the ocean floor. One was the U.S. flag. The other one was the National Geographic flag. She wanted to mark the historic spot of ocean exploration.

Several years later, while she was investigating the effects of an oil spill in Alaska, a volunteer scuba diver emerged from the water. When he was introduced to Sylvia, he simply shouted, "Jim suit!"

Sylvia was happy that people thought the dive was important. But what about all the incredible creatures she had seen? Weren't they even more extraordinary than her walk on the seafloor? When would the world share her thirst to discover not only life on other planets but the life right here on Earth?

CHAPTER 7
GUARDIAN OF THE SEA

**(Above)
Sylvia
becomes a
part of the
sea when
she dives.**

OVER THE YEARS, Sylvia had spent
thousands of hours underwater. She was always
learning something new. Her adventures
continued to attract wide attention. But she was
still not satisfied. The U.S. government and
universities were spending less, not more, on
underwater research. Sylvia was very frustrated
by this lack of interest in ocean research.

More than 70 percent of the earth is covered with water. Most of the water is in the oceans. Yet less than 1 percent of the deep sea has been explored. New marine species are constantly being discovered. With more knowledge, Sylvia was convinced that people would better understand how all life depends on the sea.

STARTING A BUSINESS

Finally, Sylvia decided she could wait no longer. She would find a way to advance ocean exploration herself. In 1981, she and engineer Graham Hawkes decided to become business partners. Their goal was to build one-person submersibles. These small vehicles could move through the ocean. They named their company Deep Ocean Technology (later called Deep Ocean Engineering).

Sylvia threw herself into the business with her usual enthusiasm. Graham Hawkes was president and chief engineer. Sylvia was vice president, secretary, and treasurer. They had little money to start up the company. So they ran the business out of Sylvia's home in Oakland, California. Discussions were ongoing. What should the submersibles be made of? Who would buy them? How could they raise money to buy supplies and pay employees? Every table was covered with business plans and drawings of subs.

Sylvia and Graham didn't have much luck selling their idea for a crewed submersible. So Graham came up with another plan. He designed a large, remotely operated vehicle (ROV). A land-based crew could send the ROV to look at undersea equipment. Finding the first customer was hard, however. Underwater technology costs a lot of money. And no one wanted to buy a new vehicle from a new company with no track record.

To Sylvia, the world of business seemed even less welcoming to women than the world of science had been. She met with businessmen to try to convince them to invest in the new company or to purchase the ROVs. But she felt they looked down on her. "In business, men generally tend not to take women very seriously. They think we don't have a brain in our heads," she said.

As the months went by, Sylvia and Graham worried that their company would fail. They finally sold one of their ROVs, named *Bandit*, to Shell Oil Company. Nine more orders followed.

Deep Rover allowed Sylvia to go to depths of the ocean that had never been explored.

In 1984, the company achieved its goal of producing a submersible that would hold people. *Deep Rover* was a small, round vehicle with mechanical arms. Made of clear acrylic, *Deep Rover* was like a sturdy bubble driven through the ocean. This was a dream come true for Sylvia. Phil Nuytten, owner of the Jim suit, bought the first one. He, Sylvia, and Graham took turns taking *Deep Rover* to 3,000 feet (914 meters). They each set a new record for solo diving.

FAMILY MATTERS

Sylvia's life was still a whirlwind. All the children were still at home. Her house and yard were always filled with animals, just as her parents' home had been. Cats, dogs, geese, lizards, parrots, horses, and guinea hens were all part of the family. Even an orphan alligator found a foster home in the backyard pool. Sylvia's father, Lewis, had died after an illness. But Sylvia's mother, Alice, often came to the house for long visits. She

Sylvia's mother *(right)* always supported her daughter's career.

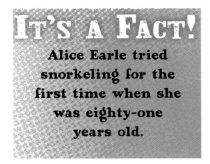

IT'S A FACT!

Alice Earle tried snorkeling for the first time when she was eighty-one years old.

brightened the serious talk with her good humor and freshly baked cookies.

After a few years, Sylvia and Graham's business partnership turned romantic. They were married in 1986. The couple decided to move the business out of their home and into a warehouse in nearby San Leandro, California. There they set up a small machine shop and testing tank.

BIG DREAMS

Business kept on improving. Graham created a smaller, easier to operate ROV called *Phantom*. *Phantom* was a big hit. One of the first customers was Walt Disney World. The theme park used *Phantom* to show visitors a fish-eye view of life inside a giant aquarium at Epcot's Living Seas Pavilion in Orlando, Florida.

Customers in more than thirty countries bought ROVs like *Phantom* to do all sorts of jobs. The submersibles found shipwrecks, checked for leaks in pipes, and dived under ice in Antarctica. A few

Graham Hawkes, Sylvia's husband, at the drawing board

police departments even used *Phantom* to search for evidence (and even dead bodies) in the ocean.

Sylvia's biggest dream was something she and Graham called Ocean Everest. Mountain climbers dream of climbing Mount Everest, the tallest peak on the land. Ocean Everest meant finding a new way to explore the deepest parts of the sea—much deeper than *Deep Rover* could go. "Ocean Everest is the code name for gaining access to our planet, from the inside out, from the ocean's greatest depths all the way back to the surface. . . , so we

Sylvia and Graham edit underwater footage that was taken with one of their submersibles.

can understand what's happening in the deep sea," she said.

A NEW JOB

Ever since Tektite, Sylvia had been frustrated. She wanted the U.S. government to pay for more sea exploration. In 1990, at the age of fifty-five, she had a chance to make this happen. President George H. W. Bush chose Sylvia to be chief scientist at the National Oceanic and Atmospheric Administration (NOAA). Sylvia felt honored to be asked. She would be the first woman ever to have the job. But she wasn't sure she wanted to accept.

In her high-level government position, she would not be able to voice her own opinions to the public. But she decided to give the job a try.

By this time, Sylvia was a well-known and respected scientist. She had spent more than six thousand hours underwater. And she held many records for her dives. Other biologists had honored her by naming species after her. These names include *Diadema sylvie*, a sea urchin, and *Pilina earli*, a red alga. The World Wildlife Fund, an important conservation organization, asked her to serve on its board of directors.

IT'S A FACT!

Sylvia has spent more than seven thousand hours of her life underwater.

Sylvia was different from most scientists, who usually become an expert in only one area. Her interests went beyond her specialty of algae. Sylvia studied the whole ecosystem (the living environment) of the ocean and its relationship to other life on earth. "She's constantly thinking, how does it all fit together, and that's a wonderful way to look at it," said shark expert Eugenie Clark.

Sylvia's new job meant she had to move to Washington, D.C. It was a good time for her to leave California. Her children were grown. Once again, her marriage had ended in divorce. She and Graham Hawkes decided to remain business partners for a few more years. Eventually they both left the company. She and her daughter Elizabeth later started a new company called Deep Ocean Exploration and Research (DOER).

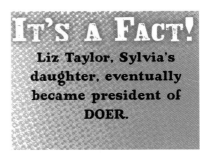

IT'S A FACT!

Liz Taylor, Sylvia's daughter, eventually became president of DOER.

DOER

Sylvia set up Deep Ocean Exploration and Research (DOER) in 1992. The company's main goals are to encourage preservation of the oceans, as well as ocean exploration. Sylvia also saw that clients who had aging underwater equipment could use DOER's experts to upgrade them. In 1997, the National Geographic Society chose DOER ROVs and submersibles in its five-year Sustainable Seas Expeditions. The company also began to develop new vehicles that used new digital technology. The company has its offices—which include a huge machine shop, a large test tank, and design facilities—in Alameda, California.

GREAT CHALLENGES

As NOAA's chief scientist, Sylvia went to many meetings and spoke before the U.S. Congress. But she also made time for expeditions. The most exciting trip came in 1991. That year, the Japanese government invited her to go on a research dive in the three-person submersible called *Shinkai 6500*. Sylvia went far deeper than she had ever gone before. She dived more than 13,000 feet (3,962 meters). This is as deep as where the *Titanic* lies.

Shinkai 6500 allowed Sylvia to go down more than 13,000 feet (3,962 meters) into the ocean—deeper than she had ever gone before.

When she returned from Japan, Sylvia was more determined than ever to persuade the U.S. government to invest money in underwater research. She knew the government spent billions of dollars on satellites that look down on the ocean. It spends a lot of money on a modern fleet of ships. But it spends only a small amount of money on the study of underwater life. She tried to make her case. But she could not get government officials to agree that sea exploration was important. In February 1992, Sylvia resigned from NOAA.

Before leaving, however, she went to the Persian Gulf region. A year earlier, the United States and its allies had fought against Saddam Hussein, the leader of Iraq. He had tried to take over Iraq's neighbor, the oil-rich country of Kuwait. After its defeat, Iraq had set fire to hundreds of oil wells in Kuwait. The fires hurt the environment terribly. Millions of barrels of oil flowed into the

IT'S A FACT!

In 1993, the U.S. Congress planned to spend $26 million for a space shuttle toilet. That year, only $19 million was marked for the country's National Underwater Research Program.

Persian Gulf. Scientists came from all over the world to study the damage. Sylvia was chief scientist of the underwater team of researchers.

When she arrived at the Persian Gulf in 1992, she found a depressing scene. The landscape was blackened for miles. Diving into slick, brown waters, she found crabs and birds smothered with black goo. Oil seeped deeply into the sand, forming an ugly pool. But she saw some reason to hope. Fresh young grass peeped through the polluted marshlands. Tiny fish found shelter in seashells. And burrowing crabs brought clean sand to the surface. Nature was struggling to heal itself.

Sylvia at the Persian Gulf

The more problems Sylvia saw in the oceans of the world, the more worried she became. Wherever she traveled, she found that life in the sea was in trouble. Trash and plastic bags from cruise ships smothered coral in the Red Sea and the Indian Ocean. Huge fishing fleets dragged enormous nets and lines in the Atlantic and Pacific Oceans. This way of fishing is called trawling. The trawling fleets took so many fish that supplies of the fish are reduced before the fish can reproduce. Chemicals and sewage wastes dumped into rivers eventually found their way to the sea. The poisons killed some plants and animals. The Gulf of Mexico that Sylvia had happily explored as a child was clouded with pollution.

"I didn't set out to be what is known as an environmentalist. But if you see things that you care about irreversibly destroyed, it's impossible not to do everything you can," she said. Sylvia would have liked nothing better than spending the rest of her life exploring the seas, swimming with whales, and identifying new critters. But she felt responsible for the world's oceans. Sylvia wanted people to understand how important it is to protect the oceans. She decided to spend more time on land, spreading her message.

HERO OF THE PLANET

Sylvia appeared on more than a hundred television programs. Many documentary films were made about her work. She spoke in sixty nations. In 1995, her book *Sea Change: A Message of the Oceans* was published. In 1996, she hosted *The Ocean Report*, a daily radio broadcast about health of the world's seas. Sylvia also wrote many magazine and journal articles. The book describes many of her adventures. Even after she became a grandmother, Sylvia's busy schedule never slowed.

The United Nations (an organization that works for world peace) and President Bill Clinton named 1998 as the Year of the Oceans. Sylvia was asked to spend the year as Explorer in Residence at the National Geographic Society. She planned to scuba dive at all of the United States' marine sanctuaries. She focused attention on the sanctuaries as one important tool for conserving life in the sea. Sylvia also started a major project in 1998. For five years, she would head an exploration called the Sustainable Seas Expeditions. During this time,

Sylvia and other scientists explored the U.S. ocean sanctuaries. The scientists studied and took pictures deep in the ocean waters.

Sylvia has written several books over the years. Many are for young readers—such as *Hello, Fish* and *Sea Critters*. In 2003 Sylvia published *Coral Reefs*. In the book, Sylvia takes readers on a journey to an "underwater city" where they can learn how coral is formed.

IT'S A FACT!

In February of 1999, Earle appeared on *Mister Rogers' Neighborhood*. The television show was taping "Noisy and Quiet." During that episode, Earle introduced a tool called a hydrophone. It let people hear noises fish make underwater.

She has also won many awards. All of the awards recognize her work to help the ocean environment. But Sylvia still feels more must be done.

In April 2005, she met with important scientists and government leaders in Barcelona, Spain. Sylvia urged the leaders to stop fishing crews from trawling to fish in the sea. Sylvia explained that trawling doesn't just kill fish. Trawling kills many animals and plants in the sea.

Sylvia herself does not eat fish. "I don't eat fish because I value them alive more than I do swimming with lemon slices and butter on my plate," says Sylvia.

Sometimes Sylvia grows discouraged about the future of the oceans. But she always finds some new reason to remain hopeful. Seeing the curiosity and excitement when she talks to children about the ocean makes her hopeful. Sylvia, now in her seventies, has four grandchildren. She is still full of energy and enthusiasm. Her busy schedule never

Sylvia poses with a granite statue of herself and the statue's sculptor, Viktor. Viktor created the sculpture to include in an underwater museum he hopes to create.

slows down. One reporter asked Sylvia what her most exciting underwater experience has been. Sylvia replied that being face-to-face with whales was at the top of her list. "But what truly makes my heart beat fastest is the knowledge that there's so much out there," said Sylvia. "It's the next adventure, always."

alga: a tiny plant usually found in water

aquanaut: a scuba diver who lives and works both inside and outside an underwater shelter for an extended period of time

bathysphere: a round steel diving machine

biologist: a scientist who studies living creatures. A marine biologist studies ocean life.

bioluminescence: light given off by living organisms

botanist: a scientist who studies plants

coral reef: a ridge made up of the skeletons of dead animals called corals

herbarium: a place where dried plant samples are kept for study and reference

marine: anything that has to do with the sea

master's degree: a further college degree after a person has earned a bachelor's degree. A student getting a master's degree specializes in a specific area of study.

National Geographic Society: a not-for-profit organization whose goal is to promote knowledge of the world among the general public. It sponsors exploration, publishes magazines, books, and bulletins, and creates television shows. The society also recently launched its own television network.

rebreather: a device that recycles air for aquanauts by removing carbon dioxide and adding oxygen from a tank as needed

role model: a person whose good behavior is copied by others

scuba: the first letters of the words self-contained underwater breathing apparatus. Scuba gear draws on a portable air supply—in scuba tanks—at a certain pressure. With the air tanks, a diver can breathe underwater.

snorkel: a tube that extends above water and makes it possible for a person to breathe while swimming facedown in the water

submersible: a small underwater craft used especially for deep-sea research

11 Wallace White, "Her Deepness," *New Yorker*, July 3, 1989, 50.

13 Sylvia Earle, interview with author, in Dunedin, FL, January 1995.

15 Alice Earle, interview with author, in Dunedin, FL, January 1995.

15–16 Sylvia Earle, interview, January 1995.

16 William Beebe, *Half Mile Down* (New York: Harcourt, Brace & Co., 1935), 10.

16 Sylvia Earle, phone interview with author, June 1995.

20 Beebe, 72.

21 Sylvia A. Earle, *Sea Change: A Message of the Oceans* (New York: G. P. Putnams Sons, 1995), 45.

24 "Sylvia Earle, Ph.D.: Undersea Explorer," *Academy of Achievement*, interview on January 27, 1991, http://www .achievement.org/autodoc/page/ ear0int-1 (September 27, 2005)

24 Sylvia Earle, interview, January 1995.

25 Sylvia Earle, interview with author in Oakland, CA, July 1995.

26 Ibid.

28 Earle, *Sea Change*, 56.

29 "An Interview with Sylvia Earle," *The Tech Museum of Innovation*, 2005, http://www .thetech.org/exhibits/online/ revolution/earle/i_c.html (September 27, 2005).

33 Ibid., 32.

34 Earle, interview, July 1995.

39 Earle, *Sea Change*, 68.

50 Earle, *Sea Change*, 70.

54 Earle, *Sea Change*, 69.

55 Sylvia Earle, interview with author in Washington, DC, October 1993.

58 Sylvia A. Earle, "Humpbacks: The Gentle Whales," *National Geographic*, January 1979, 2.

60 Ibid.

61–62 Roger Payne, phone interview with author, February 1998.

63 Ibid.

64–65 Elizabeth R. Taylor, phone interview with author, March 1998.

70 Earle, *Sea Change*, 104.

70–71 Ibid., 105.

77 Sylvia A. Earle, "A Walk in the Deep," *National Geographic*, May 1980, 629.

81 Earle, *Sea Change*, 120.

82 Earle, *National Geographic*, May 1980, 631.

83 White, 46.

86 Earle, interview, June 1995.

90–91 Earle, interview, October 1993.

92 Eugenie Clark, phone interview with author, March 1998.

97 Earle interview, July 1995.

100 "Extended Interview: Sylvia Earle," *NewsHour with Jim Lehrer*, PBS, December 2004, http://www.pbs.org/newshour/ science/coralreefs/extended_ sylvia-earle.html.

101 Josie Glausiusz, "Earle of the Sea," *Discover*, April 2000.

SELECTED BIBLIOGRAPHY

Beebe, William. *Half Mile Down*. New York: Harcourt, Brace and Co., 1935.

Carson, Rachel. *The Sea Around Us*. New York: Oxford University Press, 1989.

Clark, Eugenie. *Lady with a Spear*. New York: Harper & Brothers, 1953.

Cousteau, Jacques-Yves, with Frederic Dumas. *The Silent World*. New York: Harper and Row Publishers, 1953.

Dover, Van, and Cindy Lee. *The Octopus's Garden: Hydrothermal Vents and Other Mysteries of the Deep Sea*. Reading, MA: Addison-Wesley Publishing Co., 1996.

Earle, Sylvia. "Humpbacks: The Gentle Whales," *National Geographic*, January 1979.

Earle, Sylvia. "Life Springs from Death in Truk Lagoon," *National Geographic*, May 1976.

Earle, Sylvia. "Persian Gulf Pollution–Assessing the Damage One Year Later," *National Geographic*, February 1992.

Earle, Sylvia. "Science's Window on the Sea: All-Girl Team Tests the Habitat," pt. 2, *National Geographic*, August 1971.

Earle, Sylvia. *Sea Change: A Message of the Oceans*. New York: G. P. Putnams Sons, 1995.

Earle, Sylvia. "Undersea World of a Kelp Forest," *National Geographic*, September 1980.

Earle, Sylvia. "A Walk in the Deep," *National Geographic*, May 1980.

Earle, Sylvia A., with Al Giddings. *Exploring the Deep Frontier: The Adventure of Man in the Sea*. Washington, DC: National Geographic Society, 1980.

Payne, Roger. *Among Whales.* New York: Charles Scribner's Sons, 1995.

Piccard, Jacques, and Robert S. Dietz. *Seven Miles Down: The Story of the Bathyscaph Trieste.* New York: G. P. Putnams Sons, 1961.

FURTHER READING AND WEBSITES

Bailer, Darice. *Dive!: Your Guide to Snorkeling, Scuba, Night-Diving, Free-Diving, Exploring Shipwrecks, Caves, and More.* Washington, DC: National Geographic Society, 2002.

Briggs, Carole S. *Women Space Pioneers.* Minneapolis: Lerner Publications Company, 2005.

Dipper, Frances. *Secrets of the Deep Revealed.* New York: DK Publishing, 2003.

DuTemple Lesley A. *Jacques Cousteau.* Minneapolis: Twenty-First Century Books, 2000.

Earle, Sylvia. *Atlas of the Ocean: The Deep Frontier.* Washington, DC: National Geographic Society, 2001.

Earle, Sylvia. *Dive! My Adventures in the Deep Frontier.* New York: Scholastic, 2000.

Earle, Sylvia, and Henry Wolcott. *Wild Oceans: America's Parks Under the Sea.* Washington, DC: National Geographic Society, 1999.

Home Page for Sylvia Earle
http://literati.net/Earle/index.htm
About the author home page for Sylvia Earle. Includes links to books, book reviews, articles, and contact information.

Horsman, Paul. *Out of the Blue.* Cambridge, MA: MIT Press, 2005.

Johnson, Rebecca L. *A Journey into the Ocean.* Minneapolis: Carolrhoda Books, Inc., 2004.

Lindop, Laurie. *Venturing the Deep Sea.* Minneapolis: Twenty-First Century Books, 2006.

Mallory, Kenneth. *Swimming with Hammerhead Sharks.* Boston: Houghton Mifflin, 2001.

Marx, Christy. *Life in the Ocean Depths.* New York: Rosen Central, 2003.

Matsen, Bradford. *The Incredible Record-Setting Deep-Sea Dive of the Bathysphere.* Berkeley Heights, NJ: Enslow Publishers, 2003.

McMillan, Dianne M. *Humpback Whales.* Minneapolis: Lerner Publications Company, 2004.

National Marine Sanctuaries
http://www.sanctuaries.noaa.gov/
This site is dedicated to the marine sanctuaries of the National Oceanic and Atmospheric Administration (NOAA). It has links to each of the sanctuaries' websites, information about the NOAA, an extensive photo gallery of the various marine sanctuaries, information on conservation, and much more!

Radley, Gail. *Vanishing from Waterways.* Minneapolis: Millbrook Press, 2001.

Ross, Michael Elsohn. *Fish Watching with Eugenie Clark.* Minneapolis: Carolrhoda Books, Inc., 2000.

Souza, D. M. *Endangered Plants.* New York: Franklin Watts, 2003.

Sylvia Earle: National Geographic Explorers-in-Residence
http://www.nationalgeographic.com/council/eir/
bio_earle.html
Part of the National Geographic website, this Web page is dedicated to Sylvia Earle. It contains a brief biography, as well as links to Sustainable Seas, DOER Machine Operations, and even some of Sylvia Earle's favorite websites.

Thomas, Peggy. *Marine Mammal Preservation.* Minneapolis: Twenty-First Century Books, 2000.

Vogel, Carole Garbuny. *Human Impact.* New York: Franklin Watts, 2003.

Walker, Pam, and Elaine Wood. *People And The Sea.* New York: Facts on File, 2005.

PHOTO ACKNOWLEDGMENTS

Photographs are used with the permission of: Private collection of Sylvia Earle, pp. 4, 6, 8, 11, 14, 22, 27, 30, 32, 34, 36, 41, 42, 51, 52, 55, 63, 73, 88; Courtesy of the National Oceanic and Atmospheric Administration Central Library Photo Collection, pp. 15, 21, 57, 65; © CORBIS/Hulton-Deutsch Collection, p. 17; © OAR/National Undersea Research Program (NURP); Caribbean Marine Research Center, p. 19; © Dan Gotshall/Visuals Unlimited, p. 25; © Bettmann/CORBIS, pp. 29 (left), 43, 75; © Ed Clark/Time Life Pictures/Getty Images, p. 29 (right); Courtesy of Dr. Eugenie Clark, p. 35; © OAR/National Undersea Research Program (NURP); Black Star, Inc., p. 40; © 2005 Paul Humann/ MarineLifeImages.com, pp. 44, 79; Laura Westlund, p. 46; © OAR/National Undersea Research Program (NURP), pp. 47, 49, 72; © Chuck Savall, p. 62; © kevinschafer.com, p. 66; © Charles Nicklin/Al Giddings Images, Inc., p. 71; © Doug Perrine/SeaPics.com, p. 76; Courtesy of DOER, pp. 78, 84; © G. Musil/Visuals Unlimited, p. 80; © Jacana/Photo Researchers, Inc., p. 81; © OAR/National Undersea Research Program (NURP); Univ. of Hawaii, p. 87; © Roger Ressmeyer/CORBIS, pp. 90, 91; © OAR/National Undersea Research Program (NURP); JAMSTEC, p. 94; © Al Giddings/Al Giddings Images, Inc., p. 96; © VUAM, Courtesy of DOER, p. 100.

Front Cover: © Al Giddings/Al Giddings Images, Inc.